IN THE ZONE

GYMNASTICS

ARLENE WORSLEY

MEDIA ENHANCED BOOKS
AV2
BY WEIGL
ADDED VALUE • AUDIO VISUAL

www.av2books.com

AV² by Weigl brings you media enhanced books that support active learning.

AV² provides enriched content that supplements and complements this book. Weigl's AV² books strive to create inspired learning and engage young minds for a total learning experience.

Go to **www.av2books.com**, and enter this book's unique code. You will have access to video, audio, web links, quizzes, a slide show, and activities.

BOOK CODE

N779597

Audio
Listen to sections of the book read aloud.

Video
Watch informative video clips.

Web Link
Find research sites and play interactive games.

Try This!
Complete activities and hands-on experiments.

Due to the dynamic nature of the Internet, some of the URLs and activities provided as part of AV² by Weigl may have changed or ceased to exist. AV² by Weigl accepts no responsibility for any such changes. All media enhanced books are regularly monitored to update addresses and sites in a timely manner. Contact AV² by Weigl at 1-866-649-3445 or av2books@weigl.com with any questions, comments, or feedback.

Published by AV² by Weigl
350 5th Avenue, 59th Floor
New York, NY 10118
Website: www.av2books.com   www.weigl.com

Library of Congress Cataloging-in-Publication Data

Worsley, Arlene.
 Gymnastics : in the zone / Arlene Worsley.
    p. cm.
 Includes index.
 ISBN 978-1-60596-901-5 (hard cover : alk. paper) -- ISBN 978-1-60596-902-2 (soft cover : alk. paper) --
 ISBN 978-1-60596-903-9 (e-book)
 1. Gymnastics--Juvenile literature. I. Title.
 GV461.3.W67 2011
 796.44--dc22
                          2009050301

Printed in the United States in North Mankato, Minnesota
1 2 3 4 5 6 7 8 9   14 13 12 11 10

052010
WEP264000

PROJECT COORDINATOR   Heather C. Hudak   DESIGN   Terry Paulhus

CONTENTS

Athletes combine strength with style. Gymnastics is both a sport and an art.

Gymnastics is one of the oldest sports in the world. In Ancient Greece, children learned it in school. The Greeks believed that it was important to exercise the body as well as the mind. Gymnastics was also used to train warriors and athletes in Ancient Greece.

■ There are more than 4,000 gymnastic clubs and about three million recreational gymnasts in the United States.

Friedrich Jahn, a teacher in Germany, created modern gymnastics in 1811. He invented some of the equipment used in the sport. In 1896, the first modern Olympics were held in Athens, Greece. Gymnastics was one of nine sports that were included. It became a more popular sport in the 1970s. Gymnastics is now one of the most popular summer Olympic sports.

There are three styles of gymnastics. They are artistic, rhythmic, and trampoline gymnastics. Artistic gymnastics was introduced into the Olympics in 1896. Artistic **gymnasts** use equipment and mats in their **routines**.

Rhythmic gymnastics first appeared in the Olympic Games in 1984. Rhythmic gymnasts use balls and ribbons. They also perform to music. Sixteen years later, trampoline gymnastics were brought to the Olympics. Trampoline gymnasts do difficult flips, twists, and rolls as they bounce in the air. All three types of gymnasts must be strong and **flexible**.

Boys and girls of all ages enjoy gymnastics. Very young children like to do forward rolls. As young gymnasts grow, they learn more complex skills to match their age and abilities. Gymnastics is part of the physical education program in many elementary schools. Many high schools and colleges offer competitive gymnastic programs.

ymnasts wear stretchy, close-fitting clothing for safety and freedom of movement. Girls and women wear one-piece suits called leotards.

Boys and men wear white, sleeveless shirts with stretchy shorts or pants. Boys wear long pants for certain events. These events are the pommel horse, parallel bars, horizontal bar, and rings. Boys wear shorts for the vault and floor exercises.

Before and after performing, gymnasts wear tracksuits to keep their muscles warm. In competitions, team members wear matching uniforms.

Other gear is required to help reduce injury. Chalk powder keeps hands from slipping on the bars. Some gymnasts wear slippers, although most gymnasts prefer bare feet.

Long hair must be tied back.

Leotards are stretchy to allow gymnasts to move freely.

Rhythmic gymnasts have a different set of gear. They use ribbons, balls, hoops, ropes, and clubs in their routines. They also wear half-shoes. Half-shoes cover only the toe and ball of the foot.

When gymnasts work hard during practice or events, they **perspire**. Sweating helps the body cool down. Gymnasts keep a towel in their bag. They use it to wipe sweat from their faces and hands. They also have a water bottle filled with water. Water helps replace lost fluids due to sweating. Drinking plenty of water prevents **dehydration**.

■ During a rhythmic routine, gymnasts blend dance with acrobatics.

■ Hand grips help prevent blisters. Blisters can form when skin rubs against bars or rings.

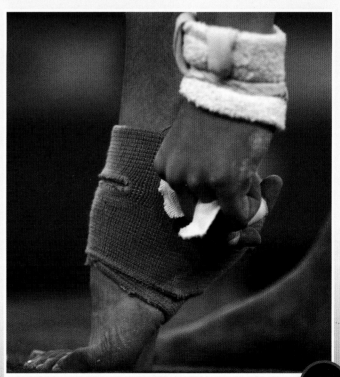

■ Some gymnasts strap their feet for extra support.

7

ymnasts need plenty of space to run, jump, and do flips, so their events take place in gymnasiums. Most gymnasiums are large with high ceilings. Gyms provide space for equipment and mats.

Sometimes, a platform is set on top of the gym floor with a layer of small springs between. These springs help gymnasts perform spins, leaps, and tumbling **moves**. Some gyms have pits that are filled with blocks of foam. When practicing **dismounts**, gymnasts land in these pits. Thick floor mats and foam pits cushion landings.

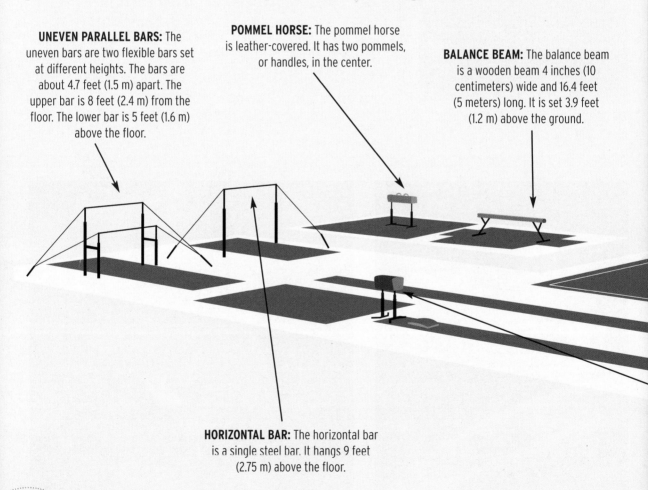

UNEVEN PARALLEL BARS: The uneven bars are two flexible bars set at different heights. The bars are about 4.7 feet (1.5 m) apart. The upper bar is 8 feet (2.4 m) from the floor. The lower bar is 5 feet (1.6 m) above the floor.

POMMEL HORSE: The pommel horse is leather-covered. It has two pommels, or handles, in the center.

BALANCE BEAM: The balance beam is a wooden beam 4 inches (10 centimeters) wide and 16.4 feet (5 meters) long. It is set 3.9 feet (1.2 m) above the ground.

HORIZONTAL BAR: The horizontal bar is a single steel bar. It hangs 9 feet (2.75 m) above the floor.

STILL RINGS: The still rings are wooden rings attached to straps. They hang about 9 feet (2.75 m) above the floor.

FLOOR: The floor mat is a large square. It measures 40 feet (12 m) by 40 feet (12 m).

PARALLEL BARS: The parallel bars are two flexible bars at the same height. The bars are 6.4 feet (1.95 m) above the ground.

VAULT: The vault includes a runway and a "horse" without handles. The runway is a long, padded mat. There is a springboard just before the horse. The "horse" is leather-covered. It measures 5 feet (1.6 m) long and 4.5 feet (1.35 m) high.

There are many **positions** and moves in gymnastics. Body positions are one of the first things gymnasts learn. The four main body positions are the pike, straddle, tuck, and layout. These positions are used in all events. They are combined with other positions and moves to produce a routine.

Gymnasts also learn different moves. Having good balance is vital for many gymnastic moves, such as the handstand. Other basic moves include the cartwheel, **somersault**, **round-off**, and forward and backward rolls. These moves are used in many events. The run-up is a few quick steps that help a gymnast gain speed during a floor or vault event.

Most coaches start gymnasts on the floor event. Gymnasts spend many hours practicing. Floor routines combine **tumbling runs** with artistic moves. Artistic moves include the round-off, handspring, and **salto**.

The endings of gymnastic routines should be controlled. There should be little to no movement when a gymnast performs a landing, such as a dismount from the vault or bars.

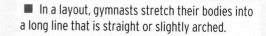
■ In a layout, gymnasts stretch their bodies into a long line that is straight or slightly arched.

Skilled gymnasts spend many hours each day practicing their routines. They have to train hard to improve their skills. A typical workout consists of three parts. They are warmups, **apparatus** practice, and **conditioning**.

Warmups are done at the beginning and at the end of a practice or performance. Gymnasts stretch, bend, and flex their bodies. It is important to stretch after the muscles have been warmed up. Stretching helps prevent injury and maintain flexibility. Some stretches include arm circles, toe touches, and neck stretches.

After warming up and stretching, gymnasts practice their routines on their apparatus. Then, the rest of the time is spent on conditioning. Conditioning includes push-ups, sit-ups, splits, and running. These activities help gymnasts increase their strength and flexibility.

■ A gymnast must have plenty of upper body strength to be successful at parallel bars.

■ Gymnasts must keep the rings as still as possible during their performance.

Although some gymnastics events are the same for boys and girls, others are different. For example, only females participate in rhythmic gymnastics.

Boys compete in six events: floor exercise, vault, pommel horse, rings, parallel bars, and horizontal bars. Girls compete in four events: floor exercise, vault, uneven parallel bars, and balance beam. Males and females have three events in common: floor exercise, vault, and parallel bars. However, there are differences in how they perform these events.

Boys and girls perform different styles of floor routines. Girls' routines are set to music. They focus on dance and tumbling. Boys' routines focus on strength, balance, and tumbling.

Boys and girls both use the vault, but they position it differently. Boys vault over it lengthwise, while girls position it sideways.

Parallel bars for boys are set side by side. Girls compete in uneven parallel bars. One bar is higher than the other. Only girls compete in balance beam, and only boys use the pommel horse, rings, and horizontal bar.

■ In the uneven bars event, gymnasts launch themselves from one bar to another bar that is more than 2 feet (61 cm) higher.

■ Gymnasts run, jump, turn, and flip on the balance beam.

It takes years of practice to become a skilled gymnast. Some gymnasts enter the sport at about eight years of age. Most gymnastics clubs offer some programs just for fun and some for competition. These programs prepare students to perform in front of people. Gymnasts usually take lessons at gymnastics clubs.

When students are ready to compete, there are many opportunities. There are about 85,000 competitive gymnasts in the United States. There are many different levels of competition.

The United States Gymnastics Foundation (USGF) sponsors gymnastics meets at the local, state, and national levels. More than 4,000 clubs in the United States offer gymnastics lessons and competitive teams. Many schools and colleges also have competitive gymnastics teams. Gymnasts compete against other gymnasts at the same level and in the same age group. There are many competition levels, from beginner to **elite**.

■ American gymnasts Nastia Liukin (left) and Shawn Johnson (right) both won medals at the Beijing 2008 Olympic Games. Liukin won silver, while Johnson won gold. Cheng Fei of China won the bronze medal.

Elite gymnasts compete at international meets and the Olympics. There are five to seven members on an Olympic gymnastics team. The U.S. national teams are chosen from 300 elite gymnasts.

Important gymnastics meets include the Olympic Games and the World Championships. At major events, there are as many as six judges. Each event has a set of required routines. Routines must show creativity and must be exciting to watch.

At the Olympics, each artistic routine is judged on a 10-point scale. This is called a Code of Points. Points or tenths of a point are taken off for mistakes. The 10 possible points are based on the level of difficulty and the nature of the routine. Rhythmic gymnastics is judged on a 30-point scale at the highest level of international competitions. Awards are given to teams and to individuals.

■ After a gymnast's performance in an event, each judge decides on a score. The scores are then totaled, and an average is calculated for that gymnast.

The sport of gymnastics has attracted many superb athletes. They thrill fans who fill the stands or watch them on television.

Sawao Kato

BORN: October 11, 1946
REPRESENTED: Japan
EVENTS: Floor, rings, parallel and horizontal bars, pommel horse

CAREER FACTS:
- Sawao Kato is considered one of the most successful male Olympic gymnasts ever.
- In three Olympics, he won 12 medals. Eight of the medals were gold.
- Kato was inducted into the International Gymnastics Hall of Fame in 2001.

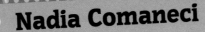

Nadia Comaneci

BORN: November 12, 1961
REPRESENTED: Romania
EVENTS: Balance beam and uneven parallel bars

CAREER FACTS:
- Comaneci was the first gymnast in Olympic history to receive a perfect score of 10. She was 14 years old.
- At the 1976 Olympic Games, she won three gold medals, a silver medal, and a bronze medal.
- In 1979, Comaneci was the first gymnast, male or female, to win a third consecutive European title.
- Comaneci helped the Romanians win their team gold medal at the World Championships in 1979.

Larisa Latynina

BORN: December 27, 1934
REPRESENTED: Soviet Union
EVENTS: Floor exercise, vault, uneven bars, balance beam

CAREER FACTS:
- Latynina has won the most medals of any athlete in Olympic history.
- Between 1956 and 1964, she won nine gold medals, five silver medals, and four bronze medals.
- At the European Championships in 1957, Latynina won all five individual events.

Kurt Thomas

BORN: March 29, 1956
REPRESENTED: United States
EVENTS: Pommel horse, floor exercise

CAREER FACTS:
- Thomas was the first U.S. male to be a serious contestant in gymnastics.
- He invented the "Thomas Flair," a twirling scissors move on the pommel horse.
- He won a gold medal at the 1978 World Championships.
- Thomas was the first gymnast to win the Sullivan Memorial Trophy. This is given to the country's top amateur athlete.

Gymnasts in the Olympics and other competitions have inspired young athletes to try this exciting sport.

Shawn Johnson

BORN: January 19, 1992
REPRESENTED: West Des Moines, Iowa
EVENTS: Balance beam, vault, uneven bars, floor exercises

CAREER FACTS:

- Johnson was named best female Olympian at the 2009 ESPY Awards after winning one gold medal and three silver medals at the Beijing Olympics.
- She is the first American female gymnast to win the Sullivan Award.
- In 2009, Johnson took part in the TV show *Dancing with the Stars*. She and her professional dance partner, Mark Ballas, won the competition.

Shannon Miller

BORN: March 10, 1977
REPRESENTED: Rolla, Missouri
EVENTS: Balance beam, uneven bars, floor exercise

CAREER FACTS:

- Miller has won seven Olympic medals and nine World Championships.
- Miller is the only American to win two straight World Championship **all-around** titles. She won them in 1993 and 1994.
- Miller was a member of the U.S. women's gymnastics team known as "The Magnificent Seven."

Vitaly Scherbo

BORN: January 13, 1972
REPRESENTED: Minsk, Belarus
EVENTS: Pommel horse, rings, horizontal bars, vault, parallel bars, floor exercise

CAREER FACTS:

- In the 1992 Summer Olympics, Scherbo became the first person ever to win four gold medals in one day.
- He was the first gymnast to win six gold medals in one Olympics.
- In 1996, he won four bronze medals in the Summer Olympics.

Nastia Liukin

BORN: October 30, 1989
REPRESENTED: Parker, Texas
EVENTS: Vault, uneven bars, balance beam, floor exercise

CAREER FACTS:

- In 2008, Liukin was the Olympic all-around Champion.
- She has won five Olympic medals.
- Liukin is a nine-time World medalist.
- She was named Women's Sports Foundation's Individual Sportswoman of the Year in 2008. Also that year, she was USA Gymnastics' Sportswoman of the Year.
- Both Liukin's parents are champions in gymnastics.

To do well in gymnastics, it is important to eat the right foods. Gymnasts must eat healthy foods and drink plenty of water. They need short bursts of energy and power in their routines.

Eating balanced meals builds strong muscles and helps athletes work hard. Foods from the **food pyramid**, such as **carbohydrates**, fruits and vegetables, protein, and milk products, contain **nutrients** needed for a healthy body. Strong bones and muscles are important when performing in an active sport, such as gymnastics.

■ Gymnasts need to drink water to keep hydrated and stay healthy.

■ Fruits and vegetables provide vitamins and minerals to keep athletes healthy.

Eating too much or too little can affect a gymnast's performance. Also, eating foods that contain large amounts of sugar leads to rapid energy swings. It is important to choose foods that are easy to digest before a gymnastics event.

Athletes need to drink water to replace what they lose when they sweat. When muscles work hard, they produce heat in the body. To keep cool, the body releases heat through sweat.

■ Gymnasts must train hard to maintain a body that is both strong and flexible. Eating a balanced diet helps gymnasts stay in shape.

Gymnastics Brain Teasers

Test your gymnastics knowledge by trying to answer these brain teasers!

1 What are the three styles of gymnastics?

2 Which Olympian was the first gymnast to ever receive a perfect score?

3 What do gymnasts wear?

4 Where do gymnastics events take place?

5 Who was the creator of modern gymnastics?

6 Name the four main body positions in gymnastics.

Glossary

all-around: a gymnast who competes in events that use all types of equipment

apparatus: the equipment used in gymnastic events

carbohydrates: foods that provide energy

conditioning: physical activities that help the body become more fit

dehydration: extreme loss of water from the body

dismounts: getting off an apparatus by trying to land on both feet

elite: very high level

flexible: able to bend easily

food pyramid: a guide used to describe healthy foods and amounts needed daily

gymnasts: athletes who participate in gymnastics

moves: certain set ways of moving the body

nutrients: substances needed by the body and obtained from food

perspire: sweat

positions: arrangement of body parts, or posture

round-off: a cartwheel move landing on both feet

routines: series of moves in a performance

salto: a flip

somersault: a forward or backward flip

tumbling runs: moves in which the gymnast runs before tumbling

Index

Log on to www.av2books.com

AV² by Weigl brings you media enhanced books that support active learning. Go to **www.av2books.com**, and enter the special code inside the front cover of this book. You will gain access to enriched and enhanced content that supplements and complements this book. Content includes video, audio, web links, quizzes, a slide show, and activities.

Audio
Listen to sections of
the book read aloud.

Video
Watch informative video clips.

Web Link
Find research sites and
play interactive games.

Try This!
Complete activities and
hands-on experiments.

WHAT'S ONLINE?

Try This! Complete activities and hands-on experiments.	**Web Link** Find research sites and play interactive games.	**Video** Watch informative video clips.	**EXTRA FEATURES**
Pages 6-7 Test your knowledge of gymnastics clothing.	**Pages 4-5** Find out more information about the history of gymnastics.	**Pages 4-5** Watch gymnasts in action. **Pages 18-19** View an interview with one of the world's top gymnasts.	**Audio** Hear introductory audio at the top of every page
Pages 8-9 See how well you know gymnastics equipment.	**Pages 8-9** Learn more about gymnastics equipment.		**Key Words** Study vocabulary, and play a matching word game.
Pages 12-13 Compare the similarities and differences between gymnastics events for males and females.	**Pages 10-11** Link to information about gymnastics moves.		**Slide Show** View images and captions, and try a writing activity.
Pages 16-17 Write a biography about one of the superstars of gymnastics.	**Pages 12-13** Read about gymnastics events for males and females.		**AV² Quiz** Take this quiz to test your knowledge
Pages 20-21 Play an interactive game.	**Pages 14-15** Learn about gymnastics competitions.		
Page 22 Test your gymnastics knowledge.	**Pages 20-21** Find out more about sports nutrition.		